AF226451

Inexplicable Magic

Inexplicable Magic

Meditation for Mystics

Susan Piver

Lionheart Press, Somerville, MA, USA
lionheartpress.net

ISBN 978-1-7369439-5-3 (paperback)
ISBN 978-1-7369439-6-0 (e-book)

Also available in audiobook.

Cover & text design by Jazmin Welch (fleck creative studio)

For the greatest magicians I ever met,
Tulku Thondup Rinpoche and Samuel Bercholz.

For the Open Heart Project and
students of magic everywhere.
I wrote this book for you.

And for Duncan, always.

Contents

INTRODUCTION

Picture this: Siddhartha Gautama (AKA Buddha Shakyamuni) has just attained complete enlightenment. After years of searching, fasting, meditating, and contemplating, getting closer and closer but never quite realizing nirvana, he decides to take a seat under a tree (now called the bodhi tree) and not rise until he pierces the veil of delusion. Which he does. He wakes up.

He rejoins his spiritual community to share with them what he discovered. There are many accounts of what he said, and those accounts have created the foundation of Buddhist thought throughout the world. He talks about the Four Noble Truths. He discusses the Middle Way. He teaches meditation. He does not say, "I've discovered a life hack, y'all" or "Meditation will make you a better leader" or "Trouble sleeping? This will help!" He makes no mention of cortisol, nor does he discuss ways to improve mental processes. Rather, I imagine he says something like, "Please try to wake up from delusion and then help others to do so. We exist within a great expanse without center or fringe, so simply open up—to yourself, others, animals, trees, the planet, everything. Meditation practice teaches just this." (I'm guessing here, as you may realize.)

The pith of the Buddha's teachings is not consonant with today's meditation trends and this short book offers a counter-reminder that this ancient and profound and absurdly simple practice has a much more soulful context. It is a practice which breaks your heart open—first to yourself, then to others, then to this world, and then, at some point, to the great bliss of abiding in the true nature. Heartbreak is among the essential seed syllables. (More on that later.)

It is wonderful, of course, that in recent years "mindfulness" has become a thing. It's important to know how to focus and pay attention in this world of surging inputs. However, it seems that something has gone awry. Rather than a path to wisdom, compassion, and bravery, mindfulness has become synonymous with stress-reduction, inner peace, and mastery. A short glance at search engine results for "mindful" reveals the mindful leader, the mindful parent, mindful sleep, football, marriage, communication, even mocktails. (Indeed, there is a book called "The Mindful Mocktail: Delicious, Nutritious Non-Alcoholic Drinks to Make at Home." Bless!)

When it comes to meditation as a spiritual practice, mindfulness is definitely part of it. But it is only half of what goes on. I posit that this mysterious other half is where the magic lies. When we sit down to meditate, we establish an uplifted posture, allow our attention to rest on the wave of breath, and let thoughts come and go (which they most certainly will do whether we "allow" them to or not). If it happens one thousand times that your attention becomes absorbed in thought rather than breath, you notice this, let go, come back, and begin again one thousand times. (See Appendix A for full instruction.) This is called mindfulness. You rest your mind on an object of your choosing (in this case, breath) and whenever you space out, you come back. That's all there is to it. In this way, you cultivate focus, precision, concentration, and…mindfulness. It's a very great thing but it really has nothing to do with parenting or mocktails. Though your increased mindfulness may enhance your capacity for patience with little ones or making a baller Cucumber-Kombucha Margarita (which actually sounds pretty good), that is not its particular purpose. It's simply a skill.

Mindfulness is the ground, not the fruition.

The other quality that meditation rouses is "awareness." This is where it gets very interesting. Meditators the world over and throughout time have reported very similar results. Sense perceptions become more vibrant. Life patterns are intuited. Hearts soften. Insights arise. In other words, awareness expands. You see more, feel more, know more. (Riddle me this: how does this happen from sitting there doing nothing? I really hope no one knows because not-knowing preserves the impenetrable mystery—and one can have ultimate confidence only in what cannot be deconstructed.)

Mindfulness can be worked at. You can read books about it, try harder, hone it more and more deeply. Awareness, however, cannot be worked at, only allowed.

In meditation practice, mindfulness and awareness are inseparable. They exist as a single enso.

Now we arrive at the secret gate. No matter how smart, learned, well-read, or well-intended you are, you cannot compel what is most desirable—love, wisdom, creative self-expression, innovation—to come to you. These are things that we receive.

They are beyond conventional thought. Otherwise we'd all be running around fully loving and wise, spewing great artworks hither and yon. But it just doesn't work that way. I mean, it can't be a coincidence that some of the worlds' greatest insights and ideas have come to people who are sleeping, showering, or walking.

Which brings me to what is probably the central point of this work on meditation as a spiritual practice:

What you seek does not come from you. It comes to you.

When we employ our meditation practice for conventional (albeit noble) aims like leading, parenting, sleeping, quelling anxiety and crafting mocktails, various studies tell us it will help. If you want these things, you could learn to meditate. But if you want to discover who you really are, deepen your capacity for intimacy, become liberated from suffering, and leap tall buildings in order to be of the greatest possible benefit to all sentient beings, you could release your agenda for this practice. Over and over. While the practice has the capacity to help you sleep better and so on, it is also custom-made for demolishing self-concept to reveal a much bigger self than you may ever have dreamed of. As it does, it cultivates the three qualities of the awakened mind, which far exceed anything you might imagine. These three qualities—remarked upon by great masters of the ages—are wisdom, compassion, and power (or bravery, if you prefer). These are the actual consequences of practice and, as such, meditation once again reveals itself as so much more than self-improvement. Spoiler: it is a way to live. And a way to die. (I digress.)

Until the mid-twentieth century, in meditation's long history it had never been suggested for solving problems or fixing our inner life, both of which have utility but no magic. It was not transactional nor meant as a method for withdrawing from the world. It was a practice to strengthen our capacity for relating, connecting, and deepening connection with the unseen elemental forces that include and extend beyond "me."

It takes courage to give up expectations for practice and step deeply into the unknown. Guardrails are required. I'm going to suggest three: the middle way; the importance of transmission, and a classical teaching called the Four Reminders. Through these three, we do what Buddhists call "establishing the view" by becoming intimate with the underlying principles and philosophies.

THE MIDDLE WAY

As mindfulness has made its way West, the inclination on the part of many teachers and practitioners has been to strip out the Buddhist-y stuff. To remove ritual, shrines, lineage, and teachings on topics like devotion. Spiritual experiences may be classified as either some kind of neurological event or steps on the path of transcendence to somewhere. Emphasis shifts solely to self-awareness as the path to non-dual awareness. Whenever I encounter someone who claims to practice non-dual awareness (or Advaita) I want to ask, "Who is practicing that?" (Once someone said to me, "I'm into non-duality" and my first thought was, *I don't think so*.) Okay, okay. All these pursuits may be worthy. But do they soften you to yourself? Do they motivate you to be more generous, disciplined, patient, and so on? Do they help you care more deeply about others? Do they accomplish anything besides staking one's own claims to spiritual attainment? (ps I'm afraid we're in an all-hands-on-deck situation here on planet Earth and if your spiritual practice doesn't contribute to peace and sanity, I'm gonna suggest you wait until another lifetime to master non-duality.)

One of the Buddha's first teachings was on the Middle Way, which posits Buddhist spiritual practice as belonging to neither of these extremes: nihilism or eternalism. Nihilism says there are no deeper meanings beyond what you can see, test, and observe. Eternalism says no, wait, there is a better place for us all. If we act right, we might get to stay there forever. I'm not saying (because I don't know) that either of these views is wrong. I'm just saying that the Buddha taught a middle way that is not nihilism, not eternalism, not neither, and not both. This is sometimes called four-fold negation (neither both nor either—nor not both and not either) but you could just as easily watch Abbott and Costello's Who's on First bit to get the feel for this four-fold negation.

There are other approaches to mindfulness that want you to be open to everyone all the time. (Ahem, bad idea). They want it to be about sweetness and light (eternalism). Then there are those who want mindfulness to be clinical and tonally cool (nihilism). You can do whatever you want, but the Buddha said "we're not doing either of those."

The middle way is also not the mid-point between the two extremes. Given this, where is it? And when the practice is not to accomplish recognition of no-self (whatever that is) or arrive at a peaceful place, what is it? Exactly.

Meditation as a spiritual practice occurs within the view of the middle way. How that happens is an unfolding mystery and you're going to have to take it from here.

TRANSMISSION QUALITY

When the practice is transmitted to you (rather than explained), it turns meditation instruction into an initiation.

By transmission, I mean the following (using myself as an example): I was taught to meditate by my meditation teacher, Sam Bercholz. He was taught by, among others, Chögyam Trungpa Rinpoche. Chögyam Trungpa was taught by people like the second Jamgön Kongtrül and Khenpo Gangshar. They were taught by their teachers who were taught by their teachers and so on, all the way back to the historic Buddha. I am in no way saying that I am sitting in for the Buddha. Trust me, I am not. However, there is an unbroken energetic line. It means… something. Who you learn from is important because you have entered the practice via a certain doorway through which many others have passed. This doesn't mean you can't walk out and go through other doorways. It's simply a factor that bears noticing. So, when you learn to meditate or get further instruction, please pay attention to the transmission quality. Transmission somehow, weirdly, conveys empowerment in practice. Is there a lineage behind your instructor and their instructions? If so, good, because we don't want any made up bullshit.

Please don't think this means you have to "become a Buddhist" or take any kind of vow. Transmission is much simpler than that. It quite simply comes, as mentioned, from a person to whom a wisdom teaching has been transmitted. If you learn a meditation practice that has been separated from its lineage, the wisdom stream dries up and its power seeks another outlet. Again, this has nothing to do with religion or belief systems. It's about getting instruction honestly come by and shared with a true intention.

THE FOUR REMINDERS

In classical Buddhist teachings, establishing and re-establishing the view is essential to approach meditation as a spiritual practice. To do so, we intentionally navigate into the unknown. There we encounter signs and signals, almost always unreadable. Unreadability is important. If they were easily understood, there would be no mystery. The more we try to "read" signs and signals within the context of habitual thought patterns, the more apt we are to increase our own confusion. There is even greater danger in turning to "experts" to interpret the signs and signals for you. (You could waste a lot of time and money that way.) Absent a true teacher (they do exist out there!), we can still be guided by true teachings.

Many sadhanas (liturgies) begin with the *Four Reminders that Turn the Mind to the Dharma*; reminders of why we're doing these practices in the first place. As mentioned, it's not about becoming a better leader, working on your problematic temper, or reducing ambient anxiety. Those things are useful but at some point your practice will invite you to go beyond them. And without Right View (the first step on the Noble Eightfold Path), you might not notice that the invitation has arrived. Cue the *Four Reminders.* They immediately reorient priorities in practice and in life.

1. "The ease and obtainments of this precious human rebirth are extremely difficult to find." Your life is precious. Singular. A shining culmination of endless life streams that came before you (AKA your parents, their parents, and so on), the culture they were raised in, the sandwiches they ate, the climates they lived in. If any one of these factors was even slightly changed, you would not be here. So it's a special situation that you're here.

2. But you won't be for long. "Whoever is born possesses the phenomena of impermanence and death." Yup. You're going to die and so is everyone else. Though I am still pretending this won't happen to me, I'm pretty sure it will happen to you. In other words, death is real.

3. "The cause and result of virtuous and non-virtuous action cannot be denied." You could try to deny it but it seems clear that everything you do plants a seed. Good seeds sprout good things. Bad seeds, well, you know the rest. *But wait,* you might reasonably then think, *shitty things happen to really great people and also the opposite is true.* The caveat with this reminder is that the seeds ripening in your life now may have been

planted in previous lifetimes and those you plant currently may not ripen until you're another being in a future lifetime. I'm not asking you to believe me or anything. But, if you think about it, this explanation makes a lot of things make sense.

4. "The continuous character of the three realms of samsara is an ocean of suffering." The three realms are desire, form, and formlessness. Going into the particulars of each realm is beyond the scope of this work, but suffice to say that each has a version of intense non-optional suffering.

The four reminders are *stark*. What do they have to do with helping me on my spiritual journey? Not hating the people I hate? Increasing compassion? Zero of the four reminders magically change me into an awesome person. However, they do change my responses, how I feel about myself, my life, and the choices I make as my day unfolds.

When I remember that my life is meaningful, precious, singular, I feel a return of awe.

When I remember that I'm going to die and so is everyone I love, including my two little cats, I feel a return of respect.

When I remember that the seeds I plant now actually mean something, I feel a return of thoughtfulness and care.

When I remember that basically none of this is going to work out, I feel a return of inspiration to break through the veils of delusion that continue to try to convince me otherwise.

Awe, respect, thoughtfulness, inspiration. These are always helpful reminders. They make you stronger and orient your practice in the right direction.

The Middle Way, the quality of transmission, and the Four Reminders support our exploration of the seven principles outlined in this work. Together, they establish the spiritual journey beyond concepts, dogma, and ambition. These principles arose out of teaching meditation and Buddhism for over a decade, most especially to my online community, the Open Heart Project. Over the years, I have observed that many practitioners struggle with how to bring the teachings into their real lives, in their everyday, in their secret lives as mystics. These principles are suggestions on just how one might do that while discovering the deepest, most mysterious and personal riches of meditation practice.

The first principle, *We Engage in Daily Ritual,* creates the ground for spiritual practice as something other than an act of self-aggression (which often accompanies efforts to improve ourselves).

The next two, *The Personal is Not an Obstacle* and *We Recognize Heartbreak* turn you inward with gentleness and courage and remind you that, as Chögyam Trungpa said, "The only true elegance is vulnerability." When we are connected to our tenderness, we are also connected to our creativity, vitality, and bravery. Rather than viewing your quirks and deep sorrows as problems to be solved, you see they are secret gates to realization.

The fourth principle, *We are Boundaried,* is meant to remind you that opening up to the mysteries and sorrows and beauties of life is not about making room for everything. Rather, paying close attention to the very personal nature of what helps or harms you is a gesture of self-respect that strengthens your capacity for love and affirms your sovereignty in everyday life.

At this point, after shoring up our personal situation to some degree, we turn our attention to the world around us, beginning with my personal favorite, *We Clean Up After Ourselves*. This may sound prosaic. It is not. When you work to not leave messes in your wake—whether in the kitchen sink or between you and a friend—you plant seeds of dignity and sanity.

The final two principles, *We Dream on Behalf of Others* and *We Live as Mystics Hiding in Plain Sight*, are about what is possible upon implementation of the previous five; you see that you are already living in a world that is inexplicably magical, a world with no division between ordinary and sacred.

To create inexplicable magic, you begin with yourself. Then you turn your heart outward. Finally, you open into an ever-widening space, beyond your concepts, ideas, hopes, and fears.

For each principle, I suggest what Buddhists call a "far and near enemy." Please note that I made up these particular enemies. The more traditional teachings on the far and near enemies are connected to the four *brahmaviharas* (or abodes): loving-kindness, compassion, sympathetic joy, equanimity.

Lastly, please don't take my word for that or anything. Investigate for yourself. This is probably the most important teaching of all. When it comes to spiritual insights and practices, the work is to apply your own intelligence to what you learn. There is only one expert who is entitled to weigh in about your experience. Though it may be disappointing to learn that you have to figure everything out yourself, it saves a lot of time and confusion to recognize it. Along the way, you will encounter many friends, some enemies, and the occasional brilliant, truly realized guru. Each can be helpful, as long as you keep paying attention to your own inner knowing and make every conceivable effort to separate true knowing from the nutty bullshit we come up with and may mistake for mastery.

A final note: This book contains insights I have gained over decades of practice with actual meditation masters. For some reason, they chose to share the deepest teachings imaginable with me. I really don't know why. If my efforts to share what I've learned with you contain errors, it is due to gaps in my understanding, not in what they taught.

WE ENGAGE IN RITUAL

FAR ENEMY: sloppiness (no form)

NEAR ENEMY: randomness (relying mostly
on ever-changing personal wishes)

Have you ever wondered why sound, rhythm, and movement are part of wisdom traditions the world over? Sufis whirl. Jews chant. Some Christian sects speak in tongues. Yogis make symbolic gestures called mudras. Tribal cultures throughout history beat drums, dance in circles, and codify certain movements to request rain, wealth, relief. Though they may be expressed in ordinary words and movements, when we assert the primacy of rhythm rather than belief, we somehow cue a different language, one that speaks in universalities rather than personal emotions and longings.

Ritual is not just rhythmic, it is rhythm itself. Day after day, recitation after recitation, incense stick after incense stick, boredom after boredom after breakthrough after sobbing…a mandala crafts itself from the rhythm of simply appearing, opening up, seeing what happens next, and letting go. Always letting go.

To establish meditation as a spiritual practice, approach it by the rhythm of ritual rather than an item on your to-do list. Ritual is key in rousing, recognizing, and emanating magic. It reminds us that we are alive and that all we do is animate; riddled with vibes.

Doubt and uncertainty are important companions along the way. It is useful to approach your rituals with questions such as: *What am I actually doing? Who is listening? What is real: what I can see or what I can feel, both or neither? Am I full of shit?* These questions provide helpful openings; they compel us into a larger space. The awareness of "how little I know" increases. This, too, is important because beyond what you know is what you seek. This is very different from the to-do list way of approaching meditation, which creates claustrophobia rather than a sense of possibility.

When meditation is shoehorned into such an environment, surely it will wither. Magic dissipates.

To continually reorient meditation away from self-improvement and toward realization, the most important factor is to contain your practice within ritual. To do so reminds you to go slower. It helps you to remember that beauty and intimacy are far more lively companions than strategies and habit trackers. Rather than taking another lap around the self-absorption track, it draws your attention to the liminal space—and this is where all the goodies reside.

Ritual calls forth liminality, richness, and magic—hallmarks of the impossible-to-trace changes that result from meditation practice. We don't know where the deepening insight, compassion, and courage come from; one day they are just there. No matter how convincing the research is on meditation, there is no study that can ever explain why you are less triggered by what normally incites, why you laugh and cry more, and why you are less tolerant of stupidity, your own and others'. Part of the reason is that you enter a different conversation with your world through your practice, one not based on *how can I fix myself/become a spiritual adept/stop crying* but on quieting down and listening in on a conversation that is already happening, all the time, between you and not-you. Though we may seek to penetrate the essence of spiritual practice by understanding its underlying concepts, the truer knowing seems to exist in the margin that is felt but unseen. Ritual is a way of relaxing into margins.

I once asked my meditation teacher, the afore-mentioned Sam, how to safeguard the spiritual nature of the practice to protect against spiritual materialism and efforts to achieve… anything. I suppose I expected some long explanation about the stages of practice or whatever. Instead, he just said, "Make offerings, request blessings, and dedicate the merit." That was it. Three things. Simple as that.

I thought, *Seriously? That's your big advice?* But over the years, I've tried it, and it actually works. These three little things can turn meditation from homework back into something that feels meaningful. And here's the thing—they're not religious, even though they might sound that way. They're just ways of remembering that meditation is about more than fixing yourself.

MAKE OFFERINGS

Before you sit, give something. It doesn't have to be fancy. Light a candle. Put some flowers on your windowsill. Play a song you love. The point is to do something generous before you ask life to be generous to you.

You can make a little shrine if you want—just a small table with things that make you happy. A photo of someone you love, a pretty stone, whatever feels right. It doesn't have to look like something from a magazine. It just has to feel like you.

Offering something concrete into the space sets the tone, but the truth is that the best offering is just being real about how you're feeling. Before you start meditating, take a minute to check in with yourself. Are you stressed? Tired? Excited? Grumpy? Whatever it is, just acknowledge it. You could even say something like, "Okay, I'm bringing my cranky Tuesday self to this practice, and that's what I have to offer today."

It sounds weird, but there's something powerful about giving your actual experience instead of trying to be the perfect meditator. You're basically saying, "This is who I am right now, and it's what I have to give."

REQUEST BLESSINGS

By the end of any ordinary day, you may find that you have mixed your mind with, say, the mind of a friend, your boss, Carl Jung, Kim Kardashian, or Steven Colbert. It all depends on what you have been exposed to in any given 24-hour period. Some exposures are intentional (you have lunch with your friend) or necessary (you meet with your boss). Some are accidental (you overhear a conversation of some sort) or anxiety inducing

(Fox News). Occasionally, we mix our minds with inexplicable beauty (John Coltrane).

It seems that many such exposures are choiceless. Sometimes they are, but in spiritual practice, you have the chance to choose who or what you wish to mix your mind with. Wisdom traditions are designed to offer such opportunities. If you walk into a Catholic church, you will be invited to mix your mind with Jesus on the cross, Mother Mary, the colors white, gold, and red. In a synagogue, you may be reminded to mix your mind with the Ten Commandments, the texts within the tabernacle, the imagined feel of certain textiles. In a Zen Buddhist temple, the invitation may be to sit with Dogen, Prajnaparamita, or… nothingness itself. A Tibetan Buddhist equivalent may introduce you to peaceful and wrathful deities and their various depictions within a kaleidoscope of colors. All you have to do to meet these sources of profundity is walk in the door.

When you sit down to meditate, with what (or whom) does your mind mix? You have choices here. Who or what inspires you, teaches you, challenges you, comforts you? Bring these sources to mind and feel their presence in some non woo-woo way. Asking them for blessings doesn't mean you have to believe in anything specific. It just means acknowledging that you're not running the whole show. Maybe there's something bigger and wiser than your individual brain at work in your life. Maybe not. But it doesn't hurt to ask.

And who are you asking? That's totally up to you. Maybe it's God, maybe it's earth spirits, maybe it's those you grieve. (As musician Nick Cave said, "We are made of ghosts, we grievers, and those spirits are forever beside us, as a protective force, part of the web of consciousness that interconnects all things.") It might be the part of you that's wiser than your everyday worrying mind. Call it whatever feels right.

The main thing is to not pretend you know exactly what you're talking about. Some mystery is good. Some not-knowing keeps things interesting.

DEDICATE THE MERIT

After you finish sitting, take a moment to notice if you feel any different. Even if it's just a tiny bit calmer or more present, acknowledge that. Then—and this is the important part—give it away.

Make a little wish that whatever good came from your practice might somehow help other people too. Your mom who's stressed about work. Your neighbor whose dog keeps barking. The person who cut you off in traffic. Everyone who might be struggling with the same stuff you are.

This isn't about being a saint. It's remembering that you're not separate from everyone else. We're all in this weird, confusing, beautiful mess together. When you feel better, it ripples out. When you're more present, it affects everyone around you.

These three things work because they shift you out of *what can I get?* mode and into *what can I give?* mode. They remind you that meditation isn't self-improvement—it's joining something bigger than yourself.

When you approach your practice like this, you stop being so uptight. Whether you're doing it right or not falls away. You stop judging your thoughts or getting frustrated when your mind wanders. You're not trying to achieve anything specific so you can relax into whatever happens.

And here's the funny thing: when you stop trying so hard to get something from meditation, you start receiving more. Not because you've earned it, but because you've made space for it. You've remembered that the point isn't to become a better person but to wake up to the person you already are. It's the difference between going to a party to network or going to a party to celebrate. Same party, totally different experience. The sacred isn't something you have to create or achieve. It's already there, waiting for you to notice.

To create the ambience of ritual, consider setting up various shrines in your home. You could have a shrine where you meditate. A shrine in your kitchen. Living room. At your bedside. It is preferred to keep them very simple. Where you practice meditation, you could have a picture of something or someone inspiring, a plant or small vase with flowers. In your kitchen, a little bowl of (uncooked) rice beneath a photo of an admired teacher; as if you could invite the teacher and the teachings to your table and into your food. By your bed, you could place objects that you associate with happiness and beauty. Please note that you can swap these objects out anytime you want. Your shrines can change with age, moods, seasons, and the state of your heart.

It seems that we are naturally drawn to creating shrines. If you look around your home, you may notice that you have already created one or two. Is there a table with pictures of loved ones? A shelf with a collection of sea glass or pretty stones? Favorite books by your bed that you read and reread, kept close as talismans or friends? This is the vibe: personal, intimate, meaningful.

THE PERSONAL IS NOT AN OBSTACLE,
IT IS THE WAY

FAR ENEMY: self-hatred (discounting your wounds, gifts, and longings)

NEAR ENEMY: self-aggression (working with self transactionally)

One of the central teachings on the Buddhist path (as well as other Eastern traditions) is the necessity of egolessness. Egolessness is another great enigma of Buddhism, difficult to articulate in large part because it is deeper and wider than any words used to describe it could possibly be. That said, many dharma geniuses have done a far better job of conveying what it is than I ever could. For example:

From the brilliant and terrifying Dzongsar Khyentse Rinpoche: *The quintessence of the path is to have the wisdom that realizes egolessness. Until we have this wisdom, we have not understood the essence of the Buddha's teaching.*

From the equally brilliant and differently terrifying Khenpo Tsultrim Gyamtso: *Because fixation on a self is the root of samsara as well as the root of karma and mental afflictions, and since fixation on the self is the root of all suffering, its opposite, selflessness, must be ascertained.*

The also brilliant and differently everything Chögyam Trungpa on egolessness: *The entire Buddhist path is based on the discovery of egolessness and the maturing of insight or knowledge that comes from egolessness.*

These are extremely trustworthy voices. They—and countless other Buddhist adepts—all say the same thing: Develop egolessness. Or else. (I added that last bit.)

The diagnosis is very clear: ego is the source of suffering. The prescription seems equally clear: transcend it. Recognize the illusion of a separate self. Realize happiness by putting others first, not self. Simple enough, except when this medicine enters the bloodstream of Western culture, something curious happens—it becomes poison. Not by its meaning, but by how it is ingested.

We Westerners arrive at the dharma pre-loaded with centuries of conditioning that whisper: *you are fundamentally flawed. The problem is you.* Our religious inheritance frequently centers on original sin, our psychological landscape is mapped according to our inadequacies, and our cultural mythology celebrates the rugged individual who pulls themself up by their bootstraps—alone, unsupported, and more or less tragic.

When the teaching "your ego is the problem" meets the Western psyche's existing conviction that "you are the problem, you have to figure it out alone, good luck," we don't get enlightenment. We get spiritually ill—a toxic cycle of self-improvement and self-hatred dressed up in dharma vocabulary.

Attempts to get rid of ego is ego pretending to try to get rid of itself. It's like punching your own self in the face expecting insight to dawn or like trying to lift yourself off the ground by pulling on your hair—theoretically interesting, practically (and dharmically) impossible.

For example, please consider these commonly suggested techniques for managing your rogue ego:

- Practice gratitude to overcome your selfish tendencies (now you're attached to being grateful)
- Put others first to transcend your self-centeredness (now you're proud of your selflessness)
- Meditate to dissolve the illusion of self (now you're a self-identified meditator)

Each solution creates its own shadow. The person who proclaims "that's just your ego" is speaking from the most defended (read: egotistic) part of themselves. The practitioner who prides herself on being egoless is virtue-signalling. This isn't failure—it's the nature of the beast. Ego cannot eliminate ego any more than darkness can eliminate itself.

Your ego isn't your enemy—it's a roadmap. Every defensive pattern, every protective strategy, every way you've learned to armor your heart arose from some kind of wisdom.

But here's the twist: this healing doesn't happen through more self-improvement. It happens through intelligent surrender— a willingness to be with what is, without immediately trying to fix, change, transcend, or learn from it.

You acknowledge the reality of your particular way of being while remaining open to the vastness that holds it.

This is where the magic happens. Not in the elimination of ego, but in the recognition that what we call "ego" and what we call "egolessness" are both movements within the same space. They are weather patterns in the same sky.

Meditation isn't self-improvement in disguise. It's not a technique for becoming someone better. It's a practice of radical receptivity—creating space for whatever arises without immediately categorizing it as spiritual or neurotic, transcendent or ordinary.

In this space of genuine receptivity, something extraordinary happens: the one who is receiving begins to dissolve into what is being received. The boundary between subject and object, between self and experience, becomes permeable. Not through effort, but through letting go.

What you discover in this dissolution or merging is what you've always been seeking: love, wisdom, authentic expression, creative flow. Rather than things you achieve, they are things you recognize as always having been there.

Here's what I want to tell my younger self and what I want to tell you: the spiritual path isn't about becoming someone else. It's about recognizing who you've always been beneath the layers of who you think you should be. Your neuroses aren't obstacles to enlightenment—they're doorways. Your wounds aren't shameful secrets to be transcended—they're unique apertures through which universal wisdom can shine. To repeat, your ego isn't the enemy—it's confused intelligence that can be befriended and transformed. Every so-called poison contains its own antidote.

As mentioned earlier, amongst the Buddha's first teaching after his awakening was about the middle way—the path between extreme asceticism and indulgence. Perhaps the middle way for contemporary practitioners is the path between spiritual bypassing and psychological fixation, between confusing transcendence with self-abandonment and endless self-improvement. This middle way asks us to hold paradox without resolving it: to work on ourselves without making that work into a form of self-aggression, to seek transcendence without abandoning our humanity, to discover egolessness without making ego the enemy.

In the end, the question isn't whether you have an ego—you do, and you always will as long as you have a human birth. The question is whether you can hold your ego lightly with humor and compassion, as one more fascinating expression of the cosmic joke that goes with pretending to have a separate existence. That holding, that lightness, that willingness to be both human and divine, neurotic and wise, wounded and whole, to *laugh* might be as close to true egolessness as any of us ever need to get.

In addition to conflating the understanding of what has personal meaning for you with egotism, eschewing the power of personal experience prevents us from detecting important patterns in our experience. There are psychological patterns, of course, but also synchronicities that seem very particular and even impossible to explain.

For example, I have a friend named Michael Carrol who is a great meditation teacher and quite possibly an even better friend. Though we have studied in the same exact tradition for decades, we did not meet at a dharma gathering. We met by coincidence at a job interview. A headhunter had suggested I meet with him to discuss a job at the publishing company where he worked. He glanced at my previous projects and all ideas about working together were subsumed in a great conversation about our practice. Okay, one great coincidence does not make a potent sense of synchronicity but fast-forward about 10 years to New York City as I stumbled out of an office building on Sixth Avenue, in tears over a horrendous, creatively disastrous meeting with my publisher (who, it turned out, hated me). I could see through my tears just enough to note that Michael Carroll, who lives in Pennsylvania, happened to be standing in front of me on Sixth Avenue for some reason I never tracked. He took one look at me and said, "Let's have lunch," whereupon he gave me great insight into my progress as a practitioner. Now it's getting interesting, right? Fast forward another few years. I'm in Boston getting ready for bed when my phone rings. *Interesting,* I thought. *Why is Michael calling me at 10p?* I answered and all I heard were muffled sounds and a few male voices. *Hello? Hello?* No one could hear me. *Pocket dial,* I thought—and indeed it was. It was also just after the moment his mother died and he and his father were talking about whether or not they should close her eyes.

Clearly, there is something potent and unknowable between me and Mikey, as I call him. Granted, it would be hard not to notice these things, but if I chalked it all up to ego or even spiritual experiences, I would be distracted from the purely intimate nature of such experiences. The personal, I hope you can see, is not an obstacle. It is the way to *something.* The mysterious nature of this "something" is also the truth of its unknowable meaning.

WE RECOGNIZE HEARTBREAK

Anyone who thinks we practice for stress-reduction, symptom-management, or improved performance is leaving the real riches on the table. However, if you practice to realize the potent power of vulnerability and heartbreak as fruits of practice, you may be well on your way to profound transformation.

Practice does not make you feel less emotional (countless depictions of peaceful meditators to the contrary). I suppose I hoped my practice would turn me into someone young, blond, and slender with a half-smile always at my lips. No offense to those who are young, blond, and slender. Some of my best friends are young, blond, and slender. I just mean that the way meditators are pictured could make one believe that youth, fairness, and tininess are the invariable results. (If I sound mocking, it is the mockery of self-knowing.)

In any case, some form of equanimity is suggested as an expected consequence of practice. After 30+ years, I can tell you that this is not an empty promise; however, this is not your grandmother's equanimity, unless granny was a non-conforming rebel who spent half her time laughing and the other half crying, usually for reasons no one else could see. Equanimous Gran (now there's an action figure I'd like to see) would probably not describe herself as peaceful, but as alive.

Alive carries its own strange peace. Rather than flattening all phenomena into an equal tone, this form of equanimity is found by embracing the full spectrum to ride the highs, lows, and in-betweens without grasping. Or, upon grasping, relinquishing the grasp on non-grasping. This is one badass Gran. If you imagine you might like to mature into such a being, one who is awake, alive, responsive, herself, you can totally do it. There is only one prerequisite: a broken heart. Though opening to heartbreak begins with opening to the realm of feeling, this opening doesn't actually have much to do with emotionality. Rather, it signals an agreement to experience what is obvious but obscured—the truth of loss.

So much confusion arises from the understandable unwillingness to feel pain. This is an unfortunate tendency in a world that contains an ocean of suffering. Everywhere you look, it's there. The first noble truth of Buddhism is commonly expressed as "Life is suffering" or "There is suffering." It has been suggested by many scholars that the word for suffering in Pali, *dukkha*, may be better translated as "unsatisfying" or even more simply as "stress." Life is unsatisfying on some very primal level.

Even that which is vastly satisfying (falling in love, accomplishing a long-held goal, seeing your garden blossom, tripping over a sack of money) ends up lacking because—and this is true 100% of the time—it dissolves. No matter how deeply you love, you will also find disappointment and loss of love, whether momentary or lasting. Achieving a wished-for outcome will not yield the expected result. Blooms fall off. Whatever you purchase with your sack of money will not actually change you or deliver on its promise. It's all unsatisfying. There is no way to get it right. Everything that arises will also fall apart.

Acknowledging this is heartbreaking. In this way, heartbreak is a threshold to seeing clearly, to liberation itself. This doesn't only mean allowing yourself to feel your own pain and the pain of others, although that is a great accomplishment. I mean the heartbreak of groundlessness, of knowing there is nothing to hold on to, absolutely nothing, and to recognize that you will never, ever get what you (think) you want. If you do, it will cease to be what you wanted. I can pretty much promise that. But this is not all that is meant by opening to heartbreak.

There is a subtle, wildly rushing river flowing incessantly, just below the surface of what is commonly held. Some people seem born into its stream, others are shocked into it, but most simply refuse it and thus their own knowing. The way in is to feel—not emotions, but currents. When you are heartbroken, suddenly you are in the choiceless position of having to feel… everything. In this way, heartbreak opens the door you try hardest to keep locked.

To work with heartbreak, three steps are required and meditation practice teaches them perfectly: precision, opening, and letting go. When you sit, the instruction is to place attention on breath. Why? Well, you're already breathing so nothing needs to be cranked up or acquired. It's deeply ordinary. This ordinariness is critical. You simply feel your body breathing.

That's the essence of the instruction. When your mind strays into thoughts and so on, you simply notice that you are thinking (no big deal), let go, and come back. That's it. Everything that is not breath is considered "thinking." It's very, very precise. Every time you notice, let go, and come back, you flex the muscle of one-pointedness. In this way, you learn how to come back to your emotional world without trying to fix the pain.

As you sit and engage in this process with curiosity, you relinquish efforts to fix yourself and simply *are* yourself. Another deeply ordinary gesture. You notice or feel that on this day, you are quiet. On that, you are speedy. Upsets of all kinds come and go, as do hopes and fears. Throughout, you simply stay. You don't get sidetracked and if you do, you see it, let go, and come back. Whatever is going on in here (barring trauma, which is its own case), is felt but not particularly thought about. This is called opening. You open to yourself, exactly as you are in this moment, not how you wish you were. You become much more gentle with your broken heart.

The third piece I've already mentioned: letting go. This may be the most profound aspect of the practice, and at the same time, it is no big deal at all. However, the capacity to notice your inner state, feel it, and then let go to come back to the present moment is probably the most powerful result of our practice. It situates you in the present and thus, magically, gives rise to clear-seeing. It softens you, first to yourself and then, again by magical means, to others. Great compassion is possible. And when you let go of working on yourself to simply be your-self trying to fix heartbreak, even if it's just for 10 minutes a day, you actually become yourself, the self who has always been there, feeling what is invisible, scared of the dark, possessed of true insight.

WE ARE BOUNDARIED

FAR ENEMY: doormat behavior ("I should be open
to everything and everyone;" shunning hierarchy as
an unkindness)
NEAR ENEMY: "good vibes only" as a lifestyle choice;
cowardice masquerading as self-care

I n spiritual circles, there is an idea that one should be tolerant and accepting of everyone and everything. Well, yeah.
When you're a Buddha I'm pretty sure this will happen
quite naturally. In the meantime, what about us non-Buddhas?
And what about those of us who were raised to put ourselves
last? The idea of boundaries—of proclaiming yourself, your
territory, your brilliance, your craziness—can feel like a form
of rudeness. If only all beings were raised to not be ashamed of
themselves and, even more importantly, to know themselves
and thus become aware of what helps and what hurts that self,
no matter what might otherwise be expected…well, it would be
easy to establish healthy boundaries.

Currently, there is a dire need for boundaries within the
incredibly divisive national dialogue (in the US and almost
everywhere) about politics, rights, and government. What can
possibly help when all the forces around us wish to sweep us
away from ourselves and into endless waves of hope and fear?

Boundaries. Boundaries allow you to protect your mind. This is of the utmost importance right now. An unprotected mind is subject to manipulations and aggression. Your meditation practice teaches you quite directly how to protect your mind by enforcing and reinforcing the skill of choosing where to place focus. This is actually what you are practicing.

Establishing proper boundaries is a consequence of knowing who you are and what you are here to do. "Here" means wherever you are right now, not any cosmic sense of purpose. For example, in many aspects of my life, I am a teacher. At this point, I've probably taught tens of thousands of people about meditation. I spend my days talking to people about their spiritual life. It is the greatest privilege of my life to do so and, to do so successfully, I must hold my seat and respect my role. It's not about knowing more than they do; I most certainly do not. It's holding the space for them to discover their own inner wisdom. I can't do this if I confuse being a teacher with being a friend or servant or professor. When I feel myself slipping off my seat, I try to pause and reposition. When I feel a student slipping off theirs (whether to move closer to me or yank the seat out from under me), same: I pause and reposition the vibe between us. Sometimes it works, sometimes it doesn't, but respect for the boundary is paramount.

When I teach retreats, as a teacher, I see that the process is happening by the changes in my students' faces. Brows relax. Eyes soften. Color returns to cheeks and lips un-purse. A general air of relaxed wakefulness replaces the rattled vigilance we all enter with. I also know it because of what they say. "I had forgotten who I was." "I remembered how to find joy." "I experienced gratitude for my life." With each passing hour, time goes even slower and the glow deepens. It is wonderful and quite surreal.

There are also moments, hours, days of sadness, remorse, or great discomfort as forgotten or resisted wounds recall themselves to each student. But somehow—and this is the magic part—the retreat container speeds fruition. They are dancing with a process and it is the dance itself that gives confidence, not any particular resolution. My work is to create the container where this can all unfold. I author the schedule, set a tone, hold the space of discipline and gentleness, and then step back while also stepping deeply in. My most important job is to respond to each moment and each student within my own heart. The work is to listen carefully, connect with what I feel, blend it with what they have said and the quality of their presence to offer something useful. To do this, my heart rides on unpredictable winds and thus the primary state for teaching well is vulnerability to one's students and one's self. It is very much a discipline.

Throughout, there is no one for me to talk with. (If there are any teachers reading this, I'm sure you understand why I say this and what it feels like.) This loneliness creates an interesting crucible, one which requires further discipline to both maintain and blend into the environment correctly. It—what I am feeling about myself, them, and the work—cannot be held separate from the work as it is the channel for connection, yet it is almost always a disaster to try to bring it in directly by referencing or explaining my own feelings.

Once, on a train from Paris to Limoge to teach a retreat at a meditation center I knew well, I learned that my sister-in-law had committed suicide. Suddenly, I went from preparing for the retreat to being a total mess, utterly confused. My initial plan was to turn right back around and fly home but I decided to proceed with my plans.

If I had said anything about this to my students, the wrong tone would have been set. However, it was impossible for me to set it aside. In between our sessions, I was online with my brother, his son, my mother, my sister, my husband, trying to stay connected and be there in whatever way I could for them and also for myself, to begin in some way to process this horrible event. In the retreat sessions, I suppose I tried to rely on my wrenched-open heart to bring benefit to the students and healing to myself. Much of it is a blur.

On the final morning, one student asked me how I felt when a retreat was over. To answer such a question is tricky. There is an important non-parity between student and teacher. It has nothing to do with superior/inferior or enlightened/unenlightened, obviously. I am absolutely no different than any of them. However, for various reasons (and because I had prepared for it due to karma and other mysteries), at this moment and for these people, I happened to hold the seat of teacher. This comes with important boundaries.

If I attempt to bring someone into my experience, problems arise. If for some reason a student tries to enter my experience, this too signals a problem and is to be assiduously avoided. So it is strange. *I am right here with you and also completely alone,* I wanted to say. This combination—right here and totally alone—is the formula for boundaries. Most of us tend to favor one end of the spectrum, whether by over-relating or withdraw-ing as a first move. Strong boundaries exist in the hinterland.

The author of *The Artist's Way*, Julia Cameron, once said, "The first rule of magic is containment." Creating something begins with establishing parameters. In this sense, boundaries become a container for magic. Without them, messy conse-quences of our actions accrue.

WE CLEAN UP AFTER OURSELVES

FAR ENEMY: letting dirt permeate everything
NEAR ENEMY: persnickety-ness and/or off-loading
all tidying

The environment in which you practice—whether your practice is meditation, love, art, or dreaming—influences and even alters the practice. You can create an environment that feeds your energy or depletes it. You are probably used to imagining yourself as contained within your body and I suppose to some degree that is true. You may also relate to environments as incidental. But just as you cannot wake up without a body, you cannot wake up without a space in which that body rests. I'm sure you've noticed that place influences mood, vitality, and flow—which must mean there's a place where "you" and environment mix with no clear fault lines.

Environments are not only the result of beautifying and organizing (both of which I love), but of attention to the details of everyday life. It sounds so persnickety to talk about this kind of expression of love and care. I believe it's difficult to talk about because of the assumed judgment, the specter of money and privilege, and the shame inherent in longing for beauty to support us. Admitting that we don't always care for ourselves and our surroundings can be really painful. We tell ourselves it doesn't matter or that we're being silly. But then, how do we explain how genuinely good we feel when we care for the containers of our life?

Right now, wherever you're sitting (assuming you are), look around. How do you feel when you do so? What details catch your attention? What would you rather not look at? I'm sitting in my living room, on the couch. I think I'm just writing (and I am), but out of the corner of my eye, I notice that my outside shoes are sort of flung about at the doorway. Apparently, I just stepped out of them as I entered and left them like that. Right now, as a rainstorm approaches central Texas, I love the soft grey hue radiating from the skylights. There are cans of flavored water on the table by the door, sent to me by mistake. What do I do with these cans? They've been sitting there for a week. Each of these little details are, on one level, vastly and truly inconsequential. At the same time, they influence me. Caring about such details, whether to tidy, repair, or appreciate, creates a sense of ambient protection and sanity. You and the environment are not separate.

In my online community, the Open Heart Project, we get together on the third Saturday of each month to co-work in silence on creative projects in a meditative environment. We meditate for a short period and then have a few hours of personal creativity time to work on whatever project is calling, whether or not it is "important." During the personal creativity hours, you're encouraged to work, not on your to-do list, but on your want-to-do list. For most people, this means writing or drawing or imagining. There is something about doing this alone-together that uplifts. Even though each person could do their project when alone, seeing other people work on their projects (alone) seems to evoke more creativity and patience. Usually, I focus on writing but on one particular day, all I could think about was cleaning out the drawers in my bathroom. I mean, how many times a day do I go into and out of this room? On some subtle level, each entry and exit left a tiny grain of sand in my metaphoric sandal. This had been going on for months. So I decided that instead of writing, I would attend to the three offending drawers. I took out every single item, decided whether to keep or recycle, wiped each item down, dusted the inside of the drawers and replaced the items in some semblance of order. Like items with like, and so on. I tell you my friends, I opened and admired those drawers a dozen times that day. I was just so pleased by this. Details cast their own inexplicable magic. Details tended to in the environment create a sense of orderliness within. As we take care of so-called ordinary things (putting laundry away, opening mail that has accumulated, disposing of expired or broken items), something in the inner terrain relaxes and finds its own mirror-like order.

When we tend our environment with genuine care and the spacious attention that simply sees, the environment itself becomes a teacher of kindness. This is how we can approach our meditation space; not as another project to perfect, but as a place deserving of our gentle, sustained attention. Such a view cannot help but deepen our practice and draw beauty toward ourselves.

WE DREAM ON BEHALF OF OTHERS

FAR ENEMY: hopelessness

NEAR ENEMY: envisioning goodness (but only for people you like)

Recently, I was leading the daily meditation we offer in the Open Heart Project Sangha (every single day, by the way—come join us). At the end, I thanked everyone for their practice. I mentioned how important it was, not just for each individual meditator, but for the whole world. Given the utter chaos of current circumstances on planet earth, someone understandably wondered how this could possibly be true. I mean, the whole world is under fire, under water, under attack, and/or under the misconception that to attack others is required. Meditation could be seen as something one does for one's own benefit alone. How can anyone justify incessantly gazing at one's own navel while the world is in big trouble?

The way we practice meditation in the Open Heart Project might begin with the possible individual benefits, but very quickly, whether or not you signed up for this, other, more far-reaching and extra-personal benefits begin to tap you on the shoulder. Of course, this is not just for us in the OHP. Generations of practitioners and countless great (and I really mean great) masters have emphasized over and over the three qualities of the awakened mind. They are promised. They're there right now, but covered over by confusions of all kinds.

First, the awakened mind is wise. This does not mean smart or knowledgeable, it means clear. Like really, really clear. Your perceptions are on-point. Your insights are accurate. Your intuitions are on fire. It's not a mistake that meditation practice is also known as the practice of insight, clear-seeing. When you see clearly, you are not (as) hoodwinked by your own misconceptions, judgments, opinions, and so on. You're actually here. You see what is happening now. And Now. "And now," says singer-songwriter Butch Hancock, "it's now again." (I think I've worked this lyric into everything I've ever written.)

Secondly, the awakened mind is compassionate. Note: this does not mean that the awakened mind is nice. Compassion has little to do with niceness. Personally, my experiences of compassion have much more in common with searing, gut-wrenching pain than anything else. It's heartbreaking to feel the suffering of others, especially, if you ask me, when the others are animals. (NO. I can't bear it. But somehow I have to.) In any case, as your practice progresses, you slowly stop "working" on yourself to simply be with yourself. Actually, that's not even right. You slowly stop working on yourself to simply *be* yourself. The consequences of this are impossible to quantify. I know it sounds unlikely. How can sitting there "doing nothing" plant the seeds of compassion that might actually kill me because they bear such ferocious fruit? The truth is, I don't know how. But here is my theory: as we sit with ourselves, we stop trying to get anywhere. We soften toward ourselves. For whatever reason, our design dictates that with such softening toward self, we immediately soften toward others. The more we allow ourselves to feel feelings, the more we feel the feelings of others. This is very important. And quite upsetting. It turns out that compassion toward self is not separate from compassion for others. (Who knew? Besides all the Buddhas, that is.)

It's no surprise then that our individual-centric culture where every action, decision, and turning point is gauged for personal benefit, has placed meditation practice in the "good for me, full stop" category. This is important, of course. But it's as important to not stop there. The mind of meditation magically, uncannily shows the next steps to be of benefit in this world. These steps don't seem to arise from project planning or deeply held intentions. They simply become visible. They are there right now. You don't craft them. Your eyes un-cloud and you just see ways to be of benefit; you feel the more kind-hearted choice; possibilities for navigating distress without causing harm become clear. You become more and more intimate with yourself and your world. It feels organic and natural and supremely not virtue-signaling. Perceptions purify and the possibility for clarity (the basis of being of benefit) is greatly enhanced.

In Buddhist thought, compassion is described in both its relative and absolute forms. Relative compassion is what you and I might imagine; acting with love, being kind (as mentioned, this is different than being nice), caring about others' suffering. Absolute compassion, on the other hand, is synonymous with emptiness. Emptiness does not mean void. Rather, it means something more like empty of independent nature. You are not empty of me. I am not empty of you. We are interdependent and inseparable. Whatever I do to myself, I do to all of creation because I am not separate from all of creation. Neither are you. Neither is your best friend. Or your worst enemy. Absolute compassion, I suppose (not having realized it at all), seems to have something to do with dissolving all sense of boundaries. Dissolving all sense of boundaries has been equated with bliss. Once, someone asked Chögyam Trungpa what bliss felt like. "To you," he said, "it would probably feel like pain." If bliss and emptiness and absolute compassion are the Buddha's preferred mixtape, this might be why.

The third quality of the awakened mind is power. My friends, let us not fear that word. You have power. I have power. It looks like life-force, sparkiness, and confidence. Bravery is a consequence of power, as are generosity and diligence. The more power we have, the greater benefit we can create. The more power, the more ability to help others discover their own. When it comes to our meditation practice and how it creates such strength, this one is the hardest to explain. It has to do with authenticity and vulnerability as gateways of power, rather than aggression and domination. As you sit, not "working" on yourself, you get to know who you really are. You may wish you were someone else, but, well, too bad. When you give up trying to craft a personality based on self-help books, cultural norms, and social media exhortations, you see the truth. While you are just a normal person like the rest of us, at the same time, you are unique in all creation. You have your ways of doing things. You have preferences and dislikes. Your wounds affect you in particular ways. You could actually fall in love with all of this, your beauty, brilliance, and craziness. When you do, when you own yourself, and accept yourself, not only could you single-handedly tank the faux wellness and self-improvement industries, you emanate well-being. Genuineness. Fearlessness. Your willingness to be vulnerable, to look at yourself and your world, map the inner terrain, is not just good for you. It is incredibly good news for me, too. You magnetize these qualities in me, simply by your presence. Thanking you in advance.

Now I ask you: what does this world need more than individuals such as yourself who know how to see clearly and perceive the world around you accurately, are willing to feel and recognize that weirdly you are not the center of the universe, and have the confidence to be real and thereby impart to me such confidence? According to my calculations, nothing.

In addition, your wisdom, compassion, and courage give you the capacity to dream, to see what is possible. Due to traumas of all kinds, there are many among us who do not currently possess that privilege. They don't have enough space to do so. Should you have such space, you should take advantage of it for the benefit of all. There are very few who have the capacity to open to the sorrows of this world and equally hold the vision of sanity, decency, and balance. This is not bypassing. It is not hiding in manufactured positivity. It is holding the view, without which we wander endlessly in confused samsaric strategies. When we start with dreams, we shake the chains that bind us to conventionality. Too, what we cannot dream, we cannot create. Please don't lose vision.

So I say that your practice is good for the world.

When I was thinking about the qualities and consequences of our meditation practice in the Open Heart Project, the list of qualities upon which this short work is based occurred to me in about 10 seconds. I just typed them out as they arose in my mind, including "we dream on behalf of others." Then, as I do with most of my writing (and thinking and wondering), I shared it with my creative colleague, heart friend, and editor, Crystal Gandrud. She added this line to what I had written about dreaming on behalf of others: "Beings such as animals or the mentally ill or trees especially need our dreams for them." I hadn't thought of these categories but, when I read them, I started to cry. The tears of my crying then produced these thoughts: animals can't dream, I vow to liberate them. The mentally ill can't dream, I vow to heal them. Trees can't dream, I vow to comfort them. These are my actual dreams and by dreaming, here, I mean envisioning, imagining, foreseeing. I would not be able to tolerate the pain that accompanies such dreams and the distance between myself and their realization without meditation practice. And perhaps it is not true that none of these beings can dream, in which case my vows still stand and I hope they dream for me.

WE LIVE AS MYSTICS
(HIDING IN PLAIN SIGHT)

FAR ENEMY: nihilism

NEAR ENEMY: eternalism

Meditation is a spiritual endeavor, a way to see beyond conventional thoughts, aspirations, and expected outcomes—and, most important, as the foundation of a life of magic. Part of the magic is you actually don't know what is happening at any given moment. Is the practice "working"? Are you becoming enlightened? Spinning wheels? Learning anything? The truth is, whatever brings you to meditation to begin with is what you will end up with. I don't know why. It could be because instead of hastening the accomplishment of dualistic goals (which, don't get me wrong, I love!), the practice reveals over and over that such goals are in no way the point. A million life-hacky, nootropic ingesting, tech-bro influencers to the contrary, this practice will not make you into… anything. Rather, it will make you into nothing. Nothing solid or lasting, in any case. This is part of the magic.

This is not for everyone. Some days, I don't even know if it is for me. Still, somehow, I have faith. The Buddhist view of faith (which sounds religious, I know) has nothing to do with belief. Rather, it is connected to how you live in every moment. The first step on the journey to faith is simply listening. First, you hear the dharma (whatever dharma interests you). In many religious traditions, the train stops here. Just listen, memorize, take it in, and then…good luck. It is now doctrine. It arose outside of your experience, that is the tell, the difference between true knowing and adopting dogma.

According to Buddhist wisdom, though, there are two more steps to take. After hearing, you contemplate, which means you mix the teaching with your own mind and experience. You turn it over, examine it, investigate, test, wait. The way to avoid blind doctrinal adherence to something someone else once said is to listen to yourself and feel your responses in the most intimate way possible. This takes a lot of courage. Step three, if what you have verified as true or meaningful (or felt to be useful) via your own wisdom mind, you now do. "Doing it" is what is meant by faith. In this sense, faith is not constantly checking in with yesterday's playbook (no matter how brilliant) but is letting go of what you knew yesterday to see what you could know today.

How do you even know what knowing is? I don't think anyone can explain this. Something just clicks. You sense something. An intuition arises. You see clearly. It's a dialogue rather than a monologue. A part of you knows something and telegraphs it. There are those who say that such knowings stem from conversations that started before you were born and will go on after you die. Wisdom itself is making an effort to converse with you. Some people call this wisdom a teacher, a guru, or the guru principle. Some call it by the name of a god or a goddess. It matters and it doesn't matter; this conversation has been going on since jump. It's happening right now. People come up with all sorts of explanations for it and propose interpretive schematics for making the most of it all. Who knows? All I can say is that meditation practice turns up the volume on such conversations and creates the foundation for living each day by what you hear.

In some Buddhist traditions (such as the one I was trained in), engaging deeply in this conversation is known as devotion. Devotion is a two-way street. Many problems have been created when one forgets that there are two inseparable intelligences at work in the conversation. When we only seek to hear and abandon our particular responses, we become slaves.

Devotion is at the root of mystic engagement with your world. And your relationship with wisdom is the object of devotion. It is a conversation with no beginning, end, center, or fringe. It seems to exist for its own enjoyment. To strike the balance between call and response, it helps to view it as you would any conversation with a loved one. Some days, you talk a lot and don't care what the other person has to say. Other days, you just listen. Or have an even exchange. Still other days, you have no idea what to say or you realize you have completely lost the plot. What were we talking about? I have no recollection. Nonetheless, the dialogue continues. At some point you see that much as you try to control and craft your life, you can't. It has a life of its own. All you can really do is practice, dedicate, and rededicate yourself to unknowable wisdom, and then get out of the way.

Some years ago, Sam suggested I read from a profound text written by Longchen Rabjam, a revered 14th-century Tibetan sage. He said, "Just read a little bit each day. You won't understand it, but don't worry about that." Truer words were never spoken. I don't understand it at all, but not because I lack intelligence. (In this case, I'm chalking up recognition of my lack of understanding as a sign of intelligence.) I don't understand it because it comes from somewhere beyond understanding. Every morning, it's like finding a message in a bottle but the message is written in disappearing ink. I can catch a letter or a phrase every now and then, but usually not. When I read something like this: *Within the expanse of spontaneous presence is the ground for all that arises, empty in essence, continuous by nature, it has never existed as anything whatsoever, yet arises as anything at all…*I think, *Yup, don't understand,* and move on. I've been reading this book for several years. When I come to the end, I start over. I still don't understand it, my friends. However, what it continuously points to—the truth of emptiness-luminosity, for example, seems to take root in my experience. Not while I'm reading, mind you, but as I'm living, in my dreaming, and as I search. I see the words paint reality.

How do seeds like this, planted in darkness, blossom in light? It must be magic.

APPENDIX A: HOW TO MEDITATE

Before you sit, please take a moment to consider the three biggest misconceptions about meditation. I mention them here to support you to avoid them.

MISCONCEPTION #1

In order to meditate, I have to clear my mind of thought.

I really wish I knew where this came from. Your mind exists to make thought, just like your eyes exist to see, your ears to hear, and so on. Telling your mind to SHUT IT is akin to telling your eyes to stop seeing and your ears to stop hearing. I invite you to try it. You can't do it! And even if you could, it would not be that great of an accomplishment.

Instead, you could allow your mind to be exactly as it is. When you meditate, thoughts will naturally come and go—it's no big deal. We waste a lot of time wishing it was different. But when we relax with ourselves as we are, no effort to change, fix, modify, eliminate, improve, the deeper benefits of meditation begin to arise on their own. The benefits include compassion for self and others, clear seeing, and open-heartedness.

These qualities are discovered when you allow attention to rest on breath as thoughts come and go in the background. It really doesn't matter if you have a lot of thoughts or just a few. What matters is that you place your breath in the foreground and relate to thoughts as ambient background noise. When you notice that you've spaced out and have become absorbed in thought, NO BIG DEAL. Just come back to the breath.

The Tibetan word for basic meditation is "gom" which means familiarization. There is nothing to perfect here, only someone (you) to get to know.

MISCONCEPTION #2
Meditation is a form of self-help.

It is absolutely true that spiritual practices bring positive change to your sense of self, your relationships, and your quality of life. They have also been scientifically proven to make you happier (by increasing activity in the prefrontal cortex) and relieve stress (by reducing cortisol). And many, many other documented benefits. This is great, obviously. However, as mentioned at the outset, these are unlikely to be the reasons the practice was taught in the first place (although they are good explanations for why meditation feels right when we really begin to do it).

I will say it again, the greatest benefits of meditation are realized when attempts at self-improvement are abandoned in favor of accepting yourself. Buddhist nun Pema Chödrön once said that cultivating gentleness toward yourself is the single most important aspect of spiritual practice. When you draw attention away from the inner chatter that is usually grading you for everything on a scale of 1 to 10, you make space for another kind of awareness to arise: your own natural, complete, and indestructible wisdom.

When you practice, you tune into the truth of who you are rather than your thoughts about who you wish you were. You see that your life has an arc, rhyme, and pattern. In fact, your life has a life of its own. You are its guardian, not its master.

Release your agenda for meditation while you are practicing. When you're not practicing, sure, have all the agendas you want because I'm sure they're worthy. But while practicing, let them go as best you can and turn your attention to this breath, this moment, this stumble, this clearing…and allow it all to unfold. Be curious about your experience rather than expecting something from it. And remember that in meditation, "We are not trying to *get* anywhere, we are trying to *be* somewhere," as Michael Carroll says. To be here rather than constantly striving to be somewhere else, signals our willingness to discover what is beyond conventional thought.

MISCONCEPTION #3
Meditation will make you more peaceful.

Spiritual practice actually cultivates vulnerability, not impenetrability—and it is right here that all the power resides, although it might not feel that way at first.

It happens with my meditation students (as also happened with me), that at some point the question comes up: When is this going to start working? I still experience anger and fear and all the things.

Contrary to marketing and advertising depictions, meditation does not make you more peaceful, if by peaceful you mean unflappable or unperturbed or some other kind of state where everything is always okay.

Our practice may pacify our minds, not by weeding out the bad thoughts and keeping the good ones (as encouraged by the thought police), but by noticing both and not necessarily believing either one. Freed from absorption in thought, we can open to what is actually happening. Into this opening come all sorts of things, wanted and unwanted, including all our good feelings and all our painful ones, and, notably, the joy and suffering of others. The more we practice, the more open we become. The more open we become, the more we feel. The more we feel, the more vulnerable we are. The more vulnerable we are, the more loving, creative, and insightful we become.

During more conventional times, I would say that simply having a steady (or steady-ish) meditation practice is enough. It will rouse the more common results of meditation: increased awareness of being, stress-reduction, becoming more patient, less easily triggered, nicer, and so on. These are great things. But these are not conventional times and more is needed—more magic, more auspicious coincidence, more depth, more mystery, more life force, and less conventionality: the esoteric fruits of a deepening practice.

It is not just about sitting on the cushion for 5 or 10 or 45 minutes and then going into your life. Please do sit for 5 or 10 or 45 minutes; it will enrich your life. But also begin to dismantle any barriers between what you do on the cushion and what you do everywhere else. Bring the mind of meditation with you. We are seeking to discover all the ways in which our homes, relationships, jobs, money, and art are practice; everything from the way we keep house to the way we express our love to each other. In this way, we focus, not only on defeating enemies but on strengthening allies.

Once, I asked a teacher what was up with all the crying that had been accompanying my practice of late. In fact, I said, the more I practiced, the more I cried. The suffering of my fellow humans seemed untenable. Surely this couldn't be what the Buddha intended as the path to enlightenment or a helpful gift I could offer others. When it came to empathy and care for my fellow humans, wiping my nose on their sleeves did not seem like the best I could do. What was I doing wrong?

He said, "Some of the world's greatest meditators have cried a lot." This simple answer was so liberating. I thought of the world's spiritual masters and sages, like the Buddha, like Jesus, like Gandhi, and tried to picture them, not as implacable adepts who always knew what to do and say, but as human beings who cried—under the Bodhi Tree, atop the Mount of Olives, in a prison cell—for all of us. But then what? They didn't just wipe their eyes and return to their lives, hoping for the best. Somehow they were left with a greater capacity for love, not less.

This profound opening is the result of a strong and steady practice. It includes deep, painful emotions as well as boring and joyful ones. It creates the perfect circumstances for us to become a more truthful version of who we already are. We open to joy, outrage, boredom, terror, and love without losing our seat. Occasionally, we may be completely at peace, but we know that it is not the result of using our practice to withdraw from this world or control ourselves, but to fearlessly enter it, take it on completely and stabilize our hearts in the open state.

PRACTICE INSTRUCTION

Find a comfortable place to sit. If you have a meditation cushion, great. If not—or if it feels uncomfortable for any reason—a regular chair is perfectly fine. What matters most is that you feel both supported and at ease.

Body

- Meditation starts with how you sit.
- Sit upright, but not stiff. Let your spine be tall, your shoulders soft. Think of yourself like a tree—rooted but flexible, able to move gently with the wind. Feel your body settle into place, right here, right now.
- If you're on a cushion, cross your legs in front of you in a way that feels relaxed. You may need to experiment with cushion height—some people like to sit close to the ground, others need more height to feel steady.
- If you're sitting on a chair, scoot toward the front so your back isn't resting against anything, and place your feet flat on the floor. If it helps, place a cushion under your feet so your knees are slightly higher than your hips.
- Place your hands on your thighs, palms down. Let your belly and shoulders relax. Tuck your chin slightly so the back of your neck is long. Let your mouth be closed, but soft—lips

gently touching, tongue resting on the roof of your mouth. Relax your jaw.

- Keep your eyes open, with your gaze soft. Let your eyes look downward to a spot about six to eight feet in front of you. You're not staring—just letting vision mix with space.

Breath

- Now, bring your attention to your breath.
- Feel it moving in and out. There's no need to breathe a certain way—just notice the natural rhythm. Every breath is a little different. See if you can feel the texture of each one. The point here is to feel, rather than observe, the breath.

Mind

- At some point, your attention will wander from breath. You might suddenly notice you're deep in thought—planning dinner, remembering a conversation, daydreaming.
- No problem.
- When that happens, simply notice it. Then gently come back to your breath. No judgment. No need to scold yourself. Just return. It doesn't matter how often (or infrequently) you have to do this.
- You don't have to stop your thoughts; you couldn't even if you wanted to anyway. You're just learning to notice where your mind is in any given moment. Thoughts come and go,

like leaves floating by in a stream. Allow them to touch you, then drift away.

- Some thoughts may feel wonderful, others painful or boring. No matter. You can let them go. Return to the breath.
- Imagine that thoughts are like clouds in the sky. Some are bright and fluffy, others heavy and dark. But no matter how many clouds appear, the sky is always there—vast, open, and untouched. In meditation, we identify more with the sky than the clouds.

Putting It All Together

When you bring awareness to your body, you begin to feel stable. When you rest attention on breath, you may feel a sense of ease. And when you gently return from thoughts, again and again, you recognize how incredibly spacious you are.

Please choose and arrange your meditation space with care and joy so it becomes a place you wish to return to. Place your meditation cushion or chair in a spot you feel happy to be in; a part of your house that gets gorgeous light or a corner of your bedroom that is quiet and peaceful. If you like, you could have a small offering table or shrine with fresh flowers or a candle or a photo of someone or something inspiring.

*Why do we sit with our eyes open? It's much easier
to practice when my eyes are closed.*

It is "easier" for some of you to meditate with closed eyes—and if the point of meditation was to be good at meditating, we would all be sitting with our eyes shut. However, it doesn't matter if you're good at meditation (PS no one is). We are practicing being awake (much easier when your eyes are open, btw). What matters is if you know how to be good at being awake in your life, showing up genuinely, and paying attention to your inner and outer experiences—all of which is easier if you're seeing what's going on. Eyes-closed practice can have more of a sense of withdrawing. When it's over, you have to come back. But when you sit with your eyes open, you never have to come back because you never went anywhere, so there can be less of a transition between your meditation practice and your post-meditation practice (AKA the rest of your life). It's also less likely that you'll fall asleep.

It's true that the majority of mindfulness meditation techniques are done with closed eyes. Perhaps this is so because most of the books and teachings come from monastics. Early teachers of meditation in the West wore robes. Their lives were devoted to prayer, study, and contemplations. If your life was centered on such things, sitting with eyes closed would make a lot of sense. But we don't live in a world constructed around inwardness. We want to remain awake in traffic, responding to texts, making art, falling in and out of love, trying to figure out how social security works. I'm just guessing here, but these are not part of the monastic lifestyle. We need a practice that works for us as householder yogins. Emphasizing attunement to the whole wide world (rather than withdrawal from it), just seems more pragmatic.

Eyes are meant to see, ears, to hear, noses, to smell, and so on. There is no particular off switch, nor does there need to be one.

How can I push past the resistance that keeps me from meditating every day? Whether it's fear, busyness, putting it last on the list, it's always the thing that gets cut.

The first thing I suggest is to set aside the notion that "resistance" is the cause. I doubt that it is. Almost everyone has difficulty with consistency—and it is simply mathematically impossible for the vast majority of human beings who wish to meditate to be unable to do so. So what is the issue, then?

I've come to the conclusion that you need to bring three things into your practice to steady it, and normally we only include one. These three things are: Buddha, Dharma, and Sangha, also known as the three jewels. Buddha means awake, dharma means path or teaching, and sangha means community. When we sit to practice, we establish a relationship with our own wakefulness. So, jewel # 1: check. However, we tend to stop there and this is where the problems arise. If we bring in some contemplation or study by reading something or journaling about our practice (dharma), we will have jewel #2. Most important (strangely, for a solitary practice) is to find a way to meditate with others from time to time. Jewel #3, sangha, is what brings it all together.

Meditation can be very boring. Am I stuck?
Doing something wrong?

Actually, you're probably doing something right. You are slowing down. Resistance to the form is dissolving. Your mind is settling. Normally, your mind is on a zillion things at once: problems, opportunities, conversations, responsibilities, promises, disappointments, television shows, advertisements, dreams, errands, exercise, transportation, scheduling—and this is just an average day. During meditation, you ask your mind to let go of all of that and instead focus on one thing: your breath. Rather than having unending occupations, suddenly there is only this one thing. It's like giving a child a doll to play with when they are used to video games. What am I supposed to do with this? It doesn't do anything. I'm bored. Well, yes. Things just got really simple and although at first it may be agitating, at some point, you settle down. Besides, isn't it kind of interesting to see how boring most of your thoughts are? There's not really a whole lot going on in the discursive theater of your mind. The good stuff is elsewhere.

On Becoming an Alchemist: A Guide for the Modern Magician
Catherine MacCoun

Start Here Now: An Open-Hearted Guide to the Path and Practice of Meditation
Susan Piver

Shambhala: The Sacred Path of the Warrior
Chögyam Trungpa

ACKNOWLEDGEMENTS

First, gratitude always to my heart-friend and editor, Crystal Gandrud, for her brilliance, generosity, anger, encouragement, and insight into the dharma. I benefit from each, equally. I want to talk with you every day for the rest of this life and all my future lives.

Thank you to my friend-sangha: Michael Carroll, Janet Gilmore, Jimmie Dale Gilmore, Christine Kane, Kelly Lindsey, Joshua Mulder, David Nichtern, Lodro Rinzler, and Lydia Segal for your devotion to the dharma and your continued willingness to talk it all over with me.

Endless gratitude to the wonderful meditation teachers who share their wisdom with the Open Heart Project: Bridget Bailey, Maho Kawachi, Kevin Townley, Lilyán de la Vega, and Marisa Viola.

To Leanna Kristine and geneviève Okuma for tending to the OHP (and to me) with care, love, and trust in the dharma.

ABOUT THE AUTHOR

SUSAN PIVER is the New York Times bestselling author of many books, including *The Wisdom of a Broken Heart*; *The Four Noble Truths of Love: Buddhist Wisdom for Modern Relationships*; *The Buddhist Enneagram: Nine Paths to Warriorship*, and *Inexplicable Joy: On the Heart Sutra*.

A student of Buddhism since 1993, Susan graduated from a Buddhist seminary in 2004. In 2012, she founded The Open Heart Project, the world's largest online-only dharma center.

ABOUT THE OPEN HEART PROJECT

The Open Heart Project is an online dharma community created by the author to explore the ideas and practices in this book. There are many ways to participate (or lurk—introverts welcome) in programs, classes, gatherings, and conversations of all kinds with Susan and other deeply trained teachers. Please visit us at openheartproject.com to learn more.

ABOUT LIONHEART PRESS

Founded by Susan Piver and Crystal Gandrud, Lionheart Press offers books that merge Buddhism with everyday life. Wherever it takes hold, Buddhist wisdom transforms its environment, but Buddhism is also changed by its environment. That is the magical, resilient alchemy of truth. Nothing static, nothing stale.

Excerpt from *The Four Noble Truths of Love:*
Buddhist Wisdom for Modern Relationships
BY SUSAN PIVER

Some time ago, my husband, Duncan, and I were locked in a state of ongoing disagreement. This disagreement had no center, theme, object, or subject. It was more like a demonic presence. Whatever we discussed gave rise to conflict, whether it was about what time to leave for the movies, if the dishes in the dishwasher were clean or dirty, which bank to use, or if we belonged together as a couple. Once we even argued about what time it was. Even a question as simple as "Where do you want to eat dinner?" could provoke talk of divorce.

(True story: When I posed this question one night, we were driving on a country road and, for some reason, we exploded at each other. I made him pull over and let me out of the car…in France. I had no idea where we were. I didn't care—I just wanted out. I walked into a field until I got scared and went back to the car, arms folded.) When we were to go somewhere, we disagreed about what we would do once we arrived. When someone said something to us, we disagreed about what it meant. When we attempted to discuss our relationship woes, we disagreed about how to do so, where to lay blame, and how to resolve them. This went on not for days or weeks, but for months. We tried many solutions: talking, not talking, making love, avoiding each other, yelling, ignoring, and, finally, at least for me, just sobbing. Nothing worked. Every interaction ended with anger, hurt feelings, or numbness. I felt so lonely, and I am sure he did too.

What was going on? There was nothing to argue about, yet everything provoked conflict. It was dreadful, terrifying. We were afraid to go near each other. I was ready to admit defeat. I thought, I have no idea where to begin fixing this. Then a voice whispered to me: "begin at the beginning." (Why are these voices always so simple and correct? And why don't they pipe up earlier?) It continued: "at the beginning are four noble truths."

They are:

Life is suffering (because everything changes).
Grasping is the cause of suffering.
It is possible to stop suffering.
There is a path for doing so.

As a twenty-years-plus student of Buddhism, these words meant something to me. What would the dharma say about my dilemma, I wondered. Why had I never thought to examine this question in relation to my relationship? After all, my Buddhist practice and study had been an unfailing guide for two decades in all other areas of my life.

But could these ancient truths be applied to my search for a lasting relationship? I was doubtful. Since the majority of great teachers lived in monasteries or caves and turned their backs on the things of this world so that they could fully embrace the spiritual path through prayer, devotion, and unconventional-ity, I had subtly imagined that their teachings would not be relevant to my modern love-life problems. I mean, they lived in monasteries, not apartments. They meditated in forests, not on the subway. They had no spouses, possessions, jobs, or bank accounts. Yes, they taught deeply, brilliantly, piercingly about love and the sacred world of emotions, but until this moment I had never thought to apply these teachings to twenty-first-century love affairs, relationships, and heartbreak.

When I did, I found a source of profound illumination that enabled me to work with my relationship problems—not to resolve them and tie them up with neat bows, but as an unerring road map back to love and intimacy. Best of all, this road map was not useful just to me, but to my husband as well, even though he is not a Buddhist practitioner. No particular beliefs, dogmas, or practices were needed to mine this wisdom.

Excerpt from *The Buddhist Enneagram:*
Nine Paths to Warriorship
BY SUSAN PIVER

I once worked closely on creative projects with a brilliant and accomplished colleague. Every time I came up with a new idea, he immediately told me why it would never work. I left each meeting in a huff, feeling some combination of shame at my stupid ideas and anger at him for not recognizing my secret genius. Creative projects involve a lot of brainstorming, experimentation, and trial and error. There was no room for any of that. I despaired of ever finding a way to work together…until I realized he was a Six on the enneagram. Sixes are preternaturally attuned to danger. They assume a hidden threat in every situation and keep looking until they find it. The moment I saw this, I stopped telling him my ideas until they were a bit more formed and I wanted to know what could go wrong—an essential bridge to cross in any creative endeavor. Once I saw that he was the perfect person to talk to, not in the germination stage, but in the execution phase of our ideas, the agita in our dynamic fell away. I saw my previous reactions to him as rooted in my own type (Four), rather than in his responses.

This ability to distinguish between your presence and my perceptions of that presence actually has the power to change the world. When I can own my feelings as generated by me (not you), I can work with them (and you) much more skillfully to either pacify, amplify, disregard, or dismantle the situation, whichever is appropriate. Without this ability, I remain trapped on the hamster wheel of self-absorption, always chasing my right and assigning my wrong.

When our differences can be appreciated as alternative superpowers rather than personal insults, difficult dynamics fade away. We can assume our rightful roles in whatever we are doing together, whether it is about love, work, cooking dinner, or saving the planet.

This is the brilliance of the enneagram. It allows us to see ourselves and others clearly. It points the way to skillful action. It shows us how to love.

Excerpt from *Inexplicable Joy: On the Heart Sutra*
BY SUSAN PIVER

Profound and insightful books have been written about the *Prajnaparamita Sutra*, also known as *The Sutra of the Heart of Transcendent Knowledge*, or just the *Heart Sutra*. This is not one of them. Rather, it is an invitation to walk through the text with me, to be inspired, confused, frustrated, and delighted by it.

The Heart Sutra confounds. It would be easy to read it and think this is crazy, what the hell?, or, I will never understand this, or most wrongheaded of all, I think I get it. In any case, whether by impatience or arrogance, a chasm would open up between you and it.

The words themselves are both ordinary (Thus have I heard) and extraordinary (form is emptiness, emptiness also is form). One could walk away from it and consider it as an ancient text that once had meaning in a long-gone cultural context or as an unfathomable, unfunny riddle requiring great spiritual erudition to comprehend.

For all its seeming opacity, the Heart Sutra remains a central text throughout the Buddhist world, particularly in Mahayana schools of thought, including the Zen tradition. It dates back to...some date. No one can really agree. 661 BCE? 100 BCE? 700 CE? It's not completely clear. We could also consider that it has always existed, authorless, hidden to be discovered by future beings like you and me through luck, timing, or various mishaps.

In accordance with the multi-layered and impenetrable nature of the Heart Sutra, it exists in a variety of editions. The longest version is rumored to be 100,000 lines long and comprise many volumes. Another version is slightly less intimidating at only 8,000 lines long. The version I recite and discuss in this work is 43 lines long. The ultimate version is zero lines long and only one syllable: AH. It's up to you which version you'd like to study.

Right now countless beings are reciting the Heart Sutra, no matter when "right now" is for you. If we could somehow hear all the voices chanting it in this moment, the beautiful, atonal cacophony might break through all our mental delusions. Add to that all the voices who have chanted it in the past and may in the future and the entire world might awaken from its suffering. May it be so.

Musings aside, though you are reading a small work written by me, I should mention that I do not understand the Heart Sutra at all. While I have been chanting it for more than three decades, I can't say I know more than I did the first time I chanted it in 1993. I encountered it when a great meditation teacher volunteered to teach me how to meditate. I had no idea why he was willing to do this, what to expect, or even much about him—we had only met once, at a party. Something inside me said DO IT, but I was still plenty nervous. Back then, meditation was still considered strange and, as mentioned, I didn't really know him. When I went over to his house, he kindly welcomed me and asked a few questions about my interest in meditation. I have no idea what I said in response. Then we sat on cushions on the floor opposite his very beautiful shrine and he handed me a piece of paper with words printed on both sides.

"We'll chant this together before we begin. It's called the Heart Sutra. Just follow along with me and skip over the words you can't pronounce."

It began:

> Thus have I heard. Once the Blessed One was dwelling in Råjagriha at Vulture Peak Mountain, together with a great gathering of the sangha of monks and a great gathering of the sangha of bodhisattvas. At that time the Blessed One entered the samådhi that expresses the dharma called "profound illumination"…

What did these words mean and why were we saying them? Sangha, bodhisattvas, samadhi? I had no idea, but I stumbled along as suggested. Then he taught me how to meditate and we sat together. He is still my meditation teacher.

Since that day, I have chanted the Heart Sutra countless times, nearly every day. I learned what all the words meant. I have gone on retreats focused on this text and nothing else. I memorized it long ago and if you woke me tonight from a sound sleep and asked me to recite the entire thing, I absolutely could.

Though I have not gained more in the way of understanding, my relationship to the text continues to deepen in ways that cannot be deconstructed, only observed. Each time I recite it, I find something I hadn't noticed before or had simply forgotten about. On good days, certain words jump out at me and provoke a flash of insight: Oh, that must be what it means. And then it disappears. In other words, there's a continuing dialogue between me and the Heart Sutra. Should you chant it, you will enter your own dialogue. What you will discuss together, I have no way of knowing.

Relating to the Heart Sutra is a little bit like falling in love. At first, there is swooning and marveling. Over time, if we are lucky, the original connection morphs into something both less exciting and more meaningful: true intimacy. Then, just like in actual human relationships, as such intimacy deepens it becomes clear that you will never really know each other. This intimate not-knowing seems to be the hallmark of the spiritual journey.

For me, nowhere is this juxtaposition more apparent (and satisfying, confounding, surprising, disappointing, comforting—just like a real relationship) than with the Heart Sutra. I hope it will be the same for you. I urge you to stay with it.

Excerpt from *Eat to Love: A Mindful Guide to Transforming Your Relationship with Food, Body, and Life*

BY JENNA HOLLENSTEIN

Eat to Love won't help you lose weight.

There are no suggestions for slimming down, toning up, eating clean, or being your best self. This book will not tell you how to detox, cleanse, go gluten-free, or cut out sugar or carbs.

If you picked it up hoping for such advice, it might be best to put it back on the shelf and keep looking. There are plenty of other books promising quick and easy weight loss and endless happiness by doing whatever worked for the author. You might even lose a few pounds. At first. Until it stops working, becomes intolerable, and you feel horrible about yourself. So if you want to try one of those, please do. Eat to Love will be here when you come back.

Still reading?

Then you should know that while it won't help you lose weight, Eat to Love will help you lose the destructive and unfounded belief that you will only be happy, healthy, and con-fident if you achieve a certain weight. It will help you drop your shame, confusion, anxiety, and paranoia about food, eating, and living in the body you have right now. It will help you shed the suffering created by the diet culture's magical eating, and free your mind and body from its stranglehold.

What Is Eat to Love?

"Eat to love" is an expression my mom used. Usually it was when recounting a dinner she cooked for someone, and how they "threw their ears back and ate to love." To me, this meant eating with a sense of unselfconscious joy. It also implied an emotional connection with the food, whether it was a favorite childhood dish or something associated with cherished memories. The way my Uncle Rob ate corned beef and cabbage or my Aunt Min dove into a bowl of spaghetti con aglio e olio. I named my non-diet nutrition therapy practice Eat to Love with the hope that I could help women rediscover the joy inherent in eating and in being in their bodies. It was only later that I realized Eat to Love had a deeper meaning.

For many of us, eating has become fraught with worry and fear. We often eat what we think we should, and not what we want. We think wanting, in and of itself, is dangerous and wrong. Or we don't know what we want anymore because, as Caroline Knapp writes in her book Appetites, our desires have become "submerged and rerouted." The deeper meaning of Eat to Love, therefore, is to eat as a form of self-love and care. To choose foods that give us pleasure and that feel good in our bodies. To treat ourselves overall as if we deserve happiness and pleasure just as we are.

Eat to Love also means feeling comfortable inhabiting the bodies we have right now. Everything we experience between the moment we are born and the moment we die happens in our bodies. From being a vehicle of bodily functions to divine ecstasy, our bodies are there with us constantly as a vehicle and as a witness. Our bodies are intersections of race, class, gender, sexuality, and ability. They move through a world that imposes ideals and values on us based on those intersections, and so no body is ever the same or ever has the same experience. In our bodies we experience pleasure and pain, strength and weakness, illness and recovery. In our bodies we experience existential questions, deepest meaning, and spiritual awakening. Our bodies define us as separate individuals and connect us with others. Yet bodily pursuits, such as those pertaining to wellness, usually leave out our spiritual side, while spiritual pursuits, such as understanding the meaning of our lives, fail to include the body. Eat to Love recognizes that body and spirit cannot exist without each other.

Eat to Love is a call to action and a call to sanity. It brings your physical body together with your spiritual self in order to mend the separation that has alienated you from your own intelligence, pleasure, and satisfaction. It is an approach to food and body that cracks you open and connects you with what you were born knowing, as well as with the deeper values that were neglected while you counted calories, chained yourself to the scale, and watched your world, but probably not your body, get smaller and smaller. On the Eat to Love path, you are likely to find yourself thinking and being in the world differently, in part by asking how you might live your life if bodies of all different sizes, shapes, colors, ages, and levels of ability were celebrated.

For more information on Jenna Hollenstein, please visit eat2love.com

Excerpt from *Mommysattva: Contemplations for Mothers Who Meditate (Or Wish They Could)*
BY JENNA HOLLENSTEIN

In Buddhism, especially Tantric Buddhism, a harmonious balance of masculine and feminine qualities are both necessary to realize enlightenment. The Buddha is often presented as having a perfect balance of the masculine and feminine. Although we all know the imagistic representations are of a man-bodied person, if we did not know that, we might well think them images of women. This is very much on purpose as an illustrative metaphor of masculine and feminine. How these qualities unfold and express themselves in the individual and in the environment is the true foundation for waking up to reality.

During quarantine, my partner taught himself how to play the piano. Granted, his brain works differently than most and he becomes a dog with a bone whenever something is challenging and interesting. Five months in and he is playing Chopin, Pachelbel, and Handel. He has this newly acquired skill, this bucket list accomplishment, to show for the months in isolation. The pieces he plays have come to serve as the soundtrack for my loading and unloading the dishwasher, for folding the laundry, chopping garlic and onions.

It would be easy to feel aggrieved: he gets to learn and practice a glorified skill while I have to take care of everyone. (Before you hate him too much, know that he works his heinie off, pays all our bills, cooks half the time, and is the chief IT officer and travel agent in our household.) And at the same time, I deeply enjoy doing these everyday tasks. They are not the only things I do in a day, but these quotidian duties are the glue that holds it all together. I take pride in cooking for my family, cleaning up the apartment, even doing the laundry (though I'd give anything to have a washer and dryer in the apartment instead of in the basement of our building). I just wish, however, that they occupied the same overall value as piano-playing. In our productivity-obsessed culture, I have wondered, "Do I have something to show for my time in quarantine?" The answer I keep coming back to is: "That is the wrong question."

So what is the right question? It has something to do with whether and how we met the challenges of having the rug pulled out from under us again and again. It is related to our capacity to open to uncertainty and change—and how we modeled that for our kids—rather than clamping down on some sort of "project." I'm fairly certain the right questions include, "Were you there for it? Did you show up? Did you stay with it? Did you allow yourself to feel?"

Even if we personally value and derive satisfaction from whatever tasks we routinely engage in, domestic and otherwise, it matters that the larger society does not. We feel deep internal conflicts for doing the work that is viewed as menial while loftier accomplishments are prized. Or we feel the need to absorb those tasks into an even grander scheme of "doing it all" and "having it all." In the words of Michelle Obama: "That shit doesn't work." Even if we enjoy these undertakings, we can harbor resentment if we have not been given a choice about doing them, if no one else is contributing, and, for me especially, if they remain invisible and unappreciated. A mother's version of the classic John Lennon song might be: "Imagine there's no wage gap, it isn't hard to do." But seriously, imagine if hospitals and midwives handed off new mothers to the care of outpatient mental health support systems with regular check-ins.

Imagine if employment benefits packages included daycare and afterschool care. What would life be like if support groups for mothers were as plentiful, varied, and ordinary as Alcoholics Anonymous meetings—those for moms of kids with special needs, foster moms, adoptive moms, stepmoms, moms attempting to blend families with wisdom and compassion? What if mom guilt was a thing of the past, and in response to rare relapses regarding prioritizing convenience in meal prep, delegating house cleaning to family members or a paid employee, or forgetting "School pajama day", everyone invoked the now well-known phrase, "Momma, you're good." Call me a dreamer, but I'm not the only one.

For more information on Jenna Hollenstein, please visit eat2love.com

Excerpt from *Look, Look, Look, Look, Look Again:*
Buddhist Wisdom Reflected in 26 Artists
BY KEVIN TOWNLEY

Cryptographer and squid enthusiast Bruce Schneier once said, "If you think technology can solve your security problems, then you don't understand the problems and you don't understand the technology." This sentiment applies to the spiritual path as well: If you think getting rid of negativity is going to solve your problems, then you don't understand your problems and you don't understand negativity. One of the distinguishing features of Tibetan Buddhism is this: IT IS PRECISELY THE THING YOU WANT TO GET RID OF THAT YOU REQUIRE IN ORDER TO BE FREE. Sorry for shouting, but negativity and positivity are not two separate things. They are, instead, contrasting experiences of a natural vitality that gets warped relative to the degree of our own personal fixation.

My first direct exposure to Buddhism was in 1999, when my father brought me to a fundraiser in Boston where a group of Tibetan monks presented an evening of sacred dance called Cham. The Cham dancers, wearing ornate brocade robes, moved in low elliptical twirls, accompanied by rumbling trumpets, cymbals, and drums. They wore startling masks portraying three-eyed demons, deer, and other spirits, which seemed more appropriate for a heavy metal concert than a religious function. To a young actor with a macabre sensibility, it was enormously appealing. Afterwards, we joined a roomful of maroon-robed monks to receive a practice transmission from His Holiness

Drikung Kyabgön Chetsang Rinpoche. Although he spoke entirely in Tibetan, some seed lodged in my mind. Years later a friend gave me a book to read by the American Buddhist nun, Pema Chödrön. I remember that one of the chapters was called, "Hopelessness and Death." These, it turned out, were meant to be positive qualities on the spiritual path, and I remembered laughing out loud—both because it seemed such a brazen thing to say and because I knew it to be true. Still, what the heck kind of spiritual path would advocate such a crazy notion?

I discovered that Pema Chödrön was connected with the same lineage of Buddhism as the monks I saw in Boston. To a lifelong fan of mystery novels, this seemed a thread worth following. I was led from Pema Chödrön to her teacher, Chögyam Trungpa. The wisdom offered to me was access to my own mind through the simple yet profound meditation practices shikantaza and shamatha-vipashyana. To whatever degree I have experienced personal transformation in my life or am able to impart any insight in this book, it is directly related to the sitting practice of meditation and not just a theoretical pursuit of Buddhism's many intellectual riches.

Chögyam Trungpa (1939–1987) was a refugee from Tibet after the Chinese invasion of 1959 and is largely responsible for reframing ancient Buddhist wisdom for a contemporary Western audience. He is a controversial figure because, in addition to being a meditation master, he also drank heavily, used drugs, and had sex with many of his students. When I first heard of his behavior, I was a little surprised because, like, if you're a spiritual leader, shouldn't you not be doing all of the worldly things my Irish Catholic grandma said would send you to hell? Well, not exactly.

There is an ancient Indian tradition of the mahasiddha ("great achiever" in Sanskrit), who is basically a person who managed to realize their enlightened nature in the course of their everyday life. Mahasiddhas were colorful individuals whose eyebrow-raising lifestyles included, but were not limited to, alcohol abuse, prostitution, murder, and ferryboat operations. As a heavy drinker myself at the time, I found all of this highly encouraging—not because I needed to have my personal addiction condoned by long-dead Indian eccentrics, but because the stories of the mahasiddhas confirmed that my drinking habits were not fundamentally at odds with my spiritual pursuits. So how ever people try to justify or decry Chögyam Trungpa's behavior—he undeniably harmed people and quite literally saved the lives of others—I felt the freedom to explore the veracity of his teachings for myself and to incorporate what was nourishing to me and set aside what was not. Weirdly, the upshot of this was that I got sober, thanks to the teachings of a person who drank himself to death. There is some poetry in that, and more than anything else, it seems to me that Chögyam Trungpa was an artist. After all, he emphasized the arts as practice modalities with his students: calligraphy, photography, flower arranging. I mention all of this not to convince you of anything—for some, the very mention of his name is a non-starter, which I totally respect (this book is likely fully refundable)—but in the Buddhist tradition it is important to honor the lineage of the teachings, which are said to be offered from warm hand to warm hand down through the ages.

Tibetan Buddhism has a lot to say about the vibrant energies we humans encounter. These energies are visually represented in the sacred image of the mandala. Mandala is a Sanskrit word meaning, simply, "circle." Mandalas are a symbol of all states of being, meant to encapsulate all energies existent in the universe. They function a bit like sacred blueprints. The structures they suggest could be any of a wide array of assemblages—from a temple, to a community, to our own body, to the unabridged cosmos. Despite its contemporary association with "mindfulness" coloring books, the mandala is a very ancient form, rich and complex.

For more on Kevin Townley, visit kevintownley.nyc